THE ABIDING FRANCHISOR

TRACKING FRANCHISEE INSURANCE, ELIMINATING RISK, AND AVOIDING CATASTROPHE

DOUG GROVES

Internet addresses given in this book were accurate at the time it went to press.

Printed in the United States of America

Published in Hellertown, PA

Cover design by Leanne Coppola

Library of Congress Control Number available upon request

ISBN 978-1-958711-65-1

For more information or to place bulk orders, contact the author or Jennifer@ BrightCommunications.net.

To my wife, who takes care of me;
to my children, who work in the business and make everything worthwhile;
and to my staff, who put up with me on our journey!

CONTENTS

Introduction   5

1. Franchisor, Beware!   9
2. The Franchise Disclosure Document   15
3. EZCert: The Certificate Tracking Solution   20
4. Our Five-Step Process   25

Afterword   42
Appendix   44
Acknowledgments   69
About the Author   71
For More Information   73

INTRODUCTION

I got started in the insurance industry in 1982. Also, I graduated from Texas A&M with a finance degree. I went into the insurance business with a company called Republic Insurance. For a couple years, I handled claims, and I was soon recruited away by Hartford. I relocated to Austin, Texas, where I then handled insurance claims. I worked with all kinds of different agencies around the central Texas area, handling general liability, workers' compensation, property, automobile, and losses. From my early experience, I saw the whole process inside and out, and I gained a pretty good feel for what insurance agents, companies, and customers were supposed to do when filing insurance claims.

In 1984, I retired my claims ability, and I went to work for an insurance agency in Austin called Capitol City Insurance Agency. For the next 26 years, I mostly ran insurance programs for general contractors and subcontractors—situations where insurance is required between those two parties. We developed new programs of insurance for general contractors working with their subcontractors.

While working for Capitol City, I identified an unmet need: General contractors should have a mechanism or a system to track and ensure that their subcontractors were in compliance with their insurance requirements. Surprisingly, most general contractors were just acting on good faith that their subcontractors were in compliance. Of course, that wasn't always the case.

My idea for general contractors to track their subcontractors' insurance compliance wasn't very effective because one general contractor usually only has around 20 to 30 subcontractors. So, I let the concept of tracking insurance simmer on a back burner for a long time.

Then in 2010, I bought an insurance agency in Georgetown, Texas, which had a haircutting franchise customer. Let's call them Brand A. The business was struggling because not all their franchisees were complying with their insurance requirements.

Brand A was having issues because they required every franchisee to hold six types of insurance coverage: general liability, property, umbrella, auto, workers' compensation, and employment practices liability. At that time, Brand A had close to 800 franchises, so that meant they needed to track up to 4,000 different insurance certifications (policies)—each year.

Suddenly, my tracking idea sprang back to life! I realized that the relationship between a franchisor and franchisees is very similar to the way that general contractors deal with subcontractors. Franchisors require their franchisees to follow their insurance requirements, just as general contractors require their subcontractors to follow their insurance requirements. However, contractors and subcontractors do not treat each other as partners, whereas franchisors and franchisees do, which makes their relationship even more complex.

I knew that we could help Brand A track their franchisees insurances, but we needed a computer program. We presented my idea to Brand A, offering to track their insurance certificates, provide them monthly statements, and make the whole process easier for them to handle.

They accepted our proposal, and I named our new program EZCert —for "easy certification." We were off and running.

Over the past five years, we've been able to make Brand A's franchisees almost wholly compliant across the whole system while maintaining tracking of all required insurances for their franchisees.

Soon after, we realized that *every* franchisor in the United States has some sort of insurance requirements. In fact, they are spelled out in their Franchise Disclosure Document (FDD). (More on FDDs in chapter 2.) I realized that we could offer EZCert service to more franchisors.

Over the years, I've had the pleasure and privilege to work with many companies and brands. This is an unmet need because the reality is that most franchisors don't have the staff nor the money to track the insurance compliance of all of their franchisees all around the country. To make matters worse, franchisees are usually allowed to buy insurance from any provider—so the information isn't even standardized. And so, the franchisor receives different paperwork from different franchisees each year for every insurance coverage that's required. It's overwhelming.

EZCert is a staff of insurance people; we understand the language. Where it might take a franchisor a half a day to read through an insurance certificate, it takes our team a matter of minutes. Also, we are able to communicate clearly with franchisees about their insurance to ensure they're protected from litigation. All these responsibilities are our bread and butter. We love what we do, and we love helping franchisors focus on their companies—instead of on their insurance.

I wrote this book to remind franchisors like you that insurance compliance is a duty that cannot be overlooked. You must maintain documentation that your franchisees are adequately insured and that they have named you as additional insured on all their policies. Also, this book is designed to tell you about EZCert—a methodology to do this other than staffing up and running your own computer reports.

I created this book to help you better understand your insurance requirements, the importance of having your franchisees in compliance with those requirements, and how our program, EZCert can help. First, we'll talk about franchisor insurance basics, and then we'll go over our five-step EZCert process. Sprinkled through the book are real case studies of some of my Abiding Franchisors and some of my Non-Abiding Franchisors.

Here's to insuring your growing business!

CHAPTER 1
FRANCHISOR, BEWARE!

What do I know about franchisors?

My experience as a franchisor is a cautionary tale of what not to do! I have been involved from the beginning in two franchisor restaurants that due to mismanagement both failed fairly impressively due to poor management from the top and mishandling staff. Twice, I fell pretty to the pitfall of being involved in businesses over which you have no control!

One of the brands grew to more than 100 units before poor hiring of family doomed the brand. Hiring family members can work well if they have the talent to do their job, but it can pose real problems if they hired for the wrong positions. Also, the leaders had gotten away from their core talents and beliefs and forgotten who the customer was.

The other brand was doomed from the start because the majority owner was clueless about how to run an operation of 14 franchisees and would not hire competent folks to run the operation.

That said, this book is *not* about my career as a franchisor. However, it is somewhat about running a franchise system correctly, and it is about my conviction that the franchise business is a great model! Maintaining insurance compliance is one of the jobs you cannot let just happen and HOPE it is done correctly!

When your business becomes a franchise and you become a franchisor, you are essentially cloning your business. You captured lightening in a bottle, and you want to spread that across the country.

That's exciting! I like the franchise business model. I think it's a great way to grow a brand. And the brands we work with become our partners in business. Together, we're growing their brands much faster than if they were opening new locations all by themselves.

Once you decide to franchise your business, your next step is recruiting franchisees. They will then duplicate your magic to create great businesses of their own. And just as you have insurance coverage to protect yourself, your franchisees need to have insurance coverage to protect themselves--and to protect you!

The franchise world is governed by the Federal Trade Commission (FTC), which started regulating franchisors and franchisees back in 1971. The FTC requires that you begin the process of franchising your business by writing a Franchise Disclosure Document (FDD). Usually, you'll hire an attorney to write your FDD. I recommend hiring an attorney who is familiar with your type of business. When your attorney writes your FDD, he or she will also write the insurance language on behalf of the franchisor.

Your FDD discloses information about your entire business to potential franchisees. The FDD must follow a prescribed format, and it's divided into 23 sections. In each of them, you must disclose everything about your business so that perspective franchisees can understand the cost and risks associated if they buy your franchise.

A lot of elements are in the FDD, including financial performances, any rules and regulations that the franchisee must follow, and even any prior litigation against the brand.

A very important component of your FDD is the insurance requirements you set for your franchisees. Your FDD must disclose what insurance you require your franchisees to carry, the limits on that insurance, and who needs to be a named insured. (We'll talk more about the specific insurance elements of your FDD in chapter 2.)

In your franchisees' insurance policies, they must be adequately covered for all business risks that they have in their businesses. For example, a franchisee who has physical locations needs insurance to cover fire, natural disasters, etc.

You, the franchisor, must be named in all the franchisees' insurance policies in the event litigation comes after both parties—the franchisee and franchisor. This is sometimes called "additional insured endorsement," and it means that the franchisor is defended as insured under the franchisee's policies. This is because in the event of a loss at any of your franchisee's locations, when a plaintiff's attorney is suing everybody in sight, typically you will be sued right behind your franchisee. The franchisee is deemed to be lower on the totem pole than you; you are suspected to have more money.

Typically, what I have observed is in the first year of franchising, the franchisee is adequately covered because both the franchisee and the franchisor have met with their attorneys and carefully reviewed the FDD. Everybody goes to the closing table, and insurance coverages are purchased because everybody is watching what goes on during that transaction.

However, each year those insurance policies need to be renewed. But the FDD isn't revisited. So, after a year or two, franchisees often lose sight of or drift away from their requirements in their purchasing of insurance. The franchisees might fail to buy the correct liability limits. Or they might not name you the franchisor as additionally insured on the policy.

You need to be concerned about your franchisees always being properly insured. Why? The biggest reason is because your top priority is having a stable business. Your franchisees pay you royalties. In the event of a casualty loss, if your franchisee is properly insured, the business can get back up and running again, and continue making royalty payments to you.

But on the other hand, if there's a casualty loss and your franchisee is not properly insured, business is not likely to get back up and running again and cannot continue making royalty payments to you!

INSURANCE PROBLEMS

There are three main scenarios all franchisors should be concerned about:

- Uninsured franchisees
- Underinsured franchisees
- Incorrectly insured franchisees

Let's talk about each in turn. An example of an *uninsured* scenario is if you're a locksmith franchisor, and one of your franchisees didn't renew his auto insurance. He let it lapse. To make matters worse, his only assets are the vans his team drives to jobs around the roads of California. If the franchisee has a wreck, you, the franchisor, will need to defend yourself for that wreck because the franchisee is unable to do so on his own behalf. Obviously, an uninsured franchisee is unacceptable to the franchisor. You need to know whether or not your franchisees have the insurance required in your FDD.

Having *underinsured* franchisees would likely lead to a similar scenario. For example, if a franchisee had only purchased $100,000 of limits where the FDD requires $1,000,000, an accident could result in $500,000 in lawsuits. Suddenly, the franchisee will tender their policy that the court of appeals had under a $100,000 limit and then you, the franchisor, would need to pay the rest. You need to know whether or not your franchisees' insurance limits are adequate per your FDD's requirements.

As a franchisor, you need to be sure your franchisees are not *incorrectly* insured. They must have the correct insurances, such as property insurance, general liability, automobile, workers' compensation, umbrella, employment practices liability, and other specific industry insurances. For example, franchisors in the liquor industry need to take certain insurance precautions. If a franchisee does not buy liquor liability insurance or if the liquor liability insurance gets canceled, the franchisee is noncompliant. If they continue selling alcohol, the franchisor is at risk.

ENSURING COMPLIANCE

In order for any franchise to be compliant, there are several things you can do:

- Have a good attorney who understands franchises, writes defendable and thorough FDDs, and is well-versed in your industry.
- Ensure that all potential loss risks that the franchisee might encounter are covered under those policies.
- Be straightforward with your franchisees about the kinds of losses that your particular business is subject to, such as slip-and-fall claims in a restaurant.
- Be clear and concise in your FDD about what types of insurance are required, what the limits are, and who the name insured must be.
- Ensure and holdfast the requirements about the insurance requirements and the brand and the additional insured liability.
- Remember that insurance renews annually, sometimes even every six months.
- Track the insurance and maintain records. In particular, watch the dates of coverage. Just because it's all in line today doesn't mean that in 13 months the franchisee will renew their insurance.

The failure of a brand to track their franchisees' insurance becomes a problem when a franchisee is sued. Then they'll suspect that there's a bigger set of pockets on the franchisor side, and they will bring you into the litigation for failure to control, failure to monitor, or failure to correctly train your franchisee. They'll name all kinds of reasons why you should also be sued. If your franchisee has gone broke, closed their doors, or had no coverage at all, the liability can easily fall on your shoulders as the franchisor.

This is exactly what we help franchisors avoid by helping them have the appropriate insurance coverage to defend them.

The reality is that when we start working with a new franchisor, they're typically only 10 to 15 percent documented compliant. In other words, only 10 to 15 percent of their franchisees have the documentation to prove they have the required insurance coverage—and 85 to 90 percent do not! There's a world of difference between what is *actually* insured and what is *documented* that it's insured.

It's incredibly challenging to run a business—let alone a franchise. Franchisors have so much on their plates, it's easy for tracking insurance compliance of their franchisees to fall way, way down on the to-do list.

That's why I created EZCert: To verify that your franchisees are covered per your FDD requirements each year and also that you as the franchisor will get additional insured status under those policies.

A NON-ABIDING FRANCHISOR

One brand, Brand B, terminated our services, and they stopped monitoring the insurance on their franchisees. Then one of their franchisees filed for bankruptcy.

The franchisor didn't know that amid the franchisee's financial difficulties he had terminated his insurance policies. And then a former employee sued both the franchisee and the franchisor over sexual harassment that had occurred before the franchise had closed.

With no insurance policy to protect the franchisor, he ended up shouldering all of the financial responsibility of this claim, settling the loss with his assets.

Had the correct insurance policies been in place at the time of the loss, those policies would have extended to cover the Brand B franchisor. Instead, the franchisor was directly affected. That's what can happen when there's no tracking on the franchisee's insurance.

If the brand had been using EZCert, we would have notified the franchisor that the franchisee had not renewed their insurance and that they were exposed to a potential lawsuit.

CHAPTER 2
THE FRANCHISE DISCLOSURE DOCUMENT

Now that we've discussed the importance of your franchisees meeting your insurance requirements, let's focus on the how you articulate those insurance requirements in your Franchise Disclosure Document (FDD).

All franchisors are required to create an FDD. In that document will be all the information about your brand that your franchisees need to know—everything from the colors of your logo, to the hours the stores must be open, to the insurances they are required to hold.

Although FDDs can be 100, 200, or even more pages, there's nothing scary about their parts or the language that goes into them. However, it's important to work with your attorney and understand your FDD so that you can fully explain it to your franchisees and make sure they are in compliance with it—always.

The FTC regulates the sale of franchisees, and they have required franchisors to organize all of this information in FDDs since 2008. Every franchisor must put the information in their FDD into the same format—a logical, set forth fashion—so that prospective franchisees can compare the franchisor with other franchisors.

Once a new franchisee signs her franchise agreement, it is usually in effect for five to 10 years. Whatever the FDD says at the point of sale, whatever rights and responsibilities are to be received by the franchisee, those are set for the entire period of time the FDD lasts.

THE FDD SECTIONS

As I mentioned previously, your FDD will follow a set format—comprised of 23 sections. Here are the sections—including the ones that relate to insurance.

Section 1: General Information: This must include the franchisor and any predecessors or affiliates that the franchisor has. It will give a description of the company and its history. Also, the franchisor must share how long she has been in business, her competition, and any special laws, licenses, or permit requirements that pertain to the industry.

Section 2: Key People and Experience: This is where the franchisor needs to identify the business and experience of the key people of the franchisor, including owners, officers, and directors. What have they done in their past? What kind of experience do they have? How long were they in business before it became a franchise?

Section 3: Litigation History: Here the franchisor discloses all litigations that the owners have been involved with—either with franchisors or with consumers over the sale of the franchise business. All past litigation and current, ongoing litigation must be described.

Section 4: Bankruptcy: Franchisors need to disclose any bankruptcies that they've been involved with. Also any management financial issues must be disclosed.

Section 5: Initial Franchise Fee: The franchisor must describe all costs involved in starting and operating a franchise. This includes deposits, nonrefundable franchise fees, and costs for initial inventory, signs, and equipment rentals. Any ranges or factors that influence those costs get disclosed here also.

Section 6: Required Training: The franchisor must include any training expected by the franchisee and all costs associated with that, such as any advertising costs associated.

Section 7: Initial Cost(s): Section seven is a detailed breakdown of the initial costs needed to operate the franchise. This includes deposits, rent, construction, and hiring employees. It could be a total of $550,000 to operate the franchise, or it could even be $1,000,000. This info is usually described in a table format for potential franchisees to compare different franchises.

Section 8: Restrictions on Sources of Products/Service: If the franchisee needs to buy inventory from the franchisor, it should be disclosed here. If the franchisee is required to source product or inventory from a certain vendor, usually it is described here.

Section 9: Obligation(s) of the Franchisee: This is where the franchisor needs to put everything the franchisee is obligated to do.

Section 10: Financing Arrangement: This section describes any financing available for the franchisee for any cost associated with the business. Franchise fees, building, contents, or inventory financing are talked about here.

Section 11: Obligation(s) of the Franchisor: This section describes the duties or services that the franchisor is obligated to perform for the franchisee.

Section 12: Territory of Protection: The franchisor needs to explain whether the franchisee is protected for one mile, three miles, five miles, or a state. Limitations and non-limitations need to be covered here.

Section 13: Trademarks: This section will go over any trademarks, tradenames, and service names the franchisor uses.

Section 14: Patents, Copyrights, and Proprietary Info: If there are any, this section explains what rights the franchisee gets to this proprietary info.

Section 15: Obligation of Franchisee's Participation: The franchisee needs to know whether the franchise is a management-run business or an owner-run business. The info on who is supposed to be involved in the business is here.

Section 16: Restrictions on Goods and Terms: This section lists what franchisees can also do in their franchises and what they can't do.

Section 17: Renewal, Termination, and Repurchase Modification: The franchisor needs to explain expectations for any kind of changes that happen and the speed of resolution going forward. In the event of disagreements, it will say how you are going to resolve them.

Section 18: Public Figures: This section is for sales figures and related numbers. For example, if a celebrity is used to help sell the business, it will give how much was paid and for how long.

Section 19: Financial Performance Representation: Most beginning franchises do not need to address this section because newer brands do not have any history. If your franchise has earnings information, you need to share it here. Overall, franchises are not required to disclose information about who gets the income or sales. For the ones that do, there are many laws having to do with what they must disclose—like an average, high, and low.

Section 20: Outlets and Franchisee Information: This section will lay out all the locations of current franchisees.

Section 21: Financial Statements: Audited financial statements for the prior three years are in this section.

Section 22 Contracts: This is a copy of all agreements the franchisee will have to sign.

Section 23: Receipts: Here is very important information about when the prospective franchisee received the FDD and when he read the document. This controls when you can write a check.

As a franchisor, be certain a prospective franchisee closely reads your FDD, especially sections 5, 6, and 7. I cannot overemphasize this duty. New franchisees usually are governed by emotion, please keep that in check and verify that they are reading your FDD carefully.

Insurance is primarily covered in sections five, six, and seven of the FDD. This is normally where the insurance requirement of a particular franchise system will be explained to the franchisee. Franchisors must disclose all coverages required of the franchisee. This includes general liability, workers' compensation, umbrella, business interruption, and automobile, etc. In these sections, if the franchisee is required to buy the list of coverages the franchisor wants in place, that list needs to be included. The FDD requires that you name the franchisor as an additional name insured so that when any litigation happens at the franchisee's location, not only is the franchisee defended by their insurance, the franchisor will also be defended. The coverage is there to protect both parties.

Usually, franchisors don't have a designated insurance company that they require—or even recommend—their franchisees buy insurance coverage from. Franchisees are usually allowed to buy their insurance from any insurance company in their state of operations. This makes it even more difficult for franchisors to track that their franchisees' insurance is compliant with their FDD.

But what happens if they are not?

When a franchisee is out of compliance or their purchased coverage doesn't match the FDD-required coverages, usually the franchisor exacts penalties, which are also spelled out in the FDD. For example, if a franchisee has two or three strikes, the franchisor might send them a letter. But at some point, the franchisee must shut down.

CHAPTER 3
EZCERT: THE CERTIFICATE TRACKING SOLUTION

Now that we've gone over the FDD, I will share EZCert's approach and our system.

You're a franchisor! Congratulations! You've officially begun cloning your lightning in a bottle.

You've hired an attorney to write your Franchise Disclosure Document (FDD). It's all taking much longer than you want, but it is what it is, and you're providing information to prospective franchisees to get them to buy your franchise system. Every day, you need to worry about payroll, your market, your franchisees' profitability, and 1,000 other details.

You might not be worrying about your franchisees' insurances. But you should be.

You should be monitoring their insurance coverage, limits, additional insurance endorsements, and expiration dates to ensure everything is correct and current. Are you compliant? Are your franchisees?

If you have 10 franchisees, your corporate team might be able to monitor them all. But if you have hundreds of franchisees, your team probably cannot. But EZCert can!

The Origins of EZCert

We created EZCert to bring ease to tracking franchisees' certificates of insurance. Most people find it difficult to read insurance certificates.

Our insurance pros, however, in minutes can read certificates that might take an untrained person days to wade through.

The tracking of insurance certificates is a very common business. Typically, it's done between a landlord and a lessee or a general contractor and a subcontractor, but it's also done between a franchisor and franchisee. The unique part for franchisors and franchisees is that the insurance certificate and the royalty payments flow in the same direction. In other words, the franchisor requests the insurance certificate to match the FDD requirements, and the franchisor charges the franchisee royalties.

On the other hand, when a general contractor asks a subcontractor for insurance, the general contractor is paying their revenue to the subcontractor. And then, the check and the certificate of insurance actually cross in the mail. Honestly, this is a very healthy system. In the franchisor/franchisee world, the royalty check and the certificate of insurance flow the same direction. If there is a difference of opinion, if a franchisee is not covering the correct exposures that the FDD requires, if the franchisee doesn't use the right insurance company, if they don't pay their bills, or if they go broke, that insurance certificate is not going to the franchisor. This is what causes the franchisor some heartache. Now they must call their franchisee—from whom they get their royalty check—and have a frank discussion about their lack of insurance coverage.

Tracking insurance certifications for franchisors was a logical step for EZCert because our EZCert people were all formerly franchisor people. Personally, I handled franchisors and franchisees for different systems, so I knew that relationship between them. When EZCert began, I already knew about the conversations that needed to happen, and how they needed to go. Those conversations must be delicate (because the franchisee is your customer) but firm (because you have entered into a contract with your franchisee, and the franchisee guaranteed you that they would buy required insurance coverages).

As explained in my Introduction, in 2010, the importance of tracking certificates of insurance came to the forefront for EZCert when we were working with the brand mentioned in this book's introduction, Brand A, in Georgetown, Texas. A mountain of paperwork was coming in to corporate from their 800 locations. It was a management and an employee nightmare, and it did nothing to bring revenue to Brand A. Each week, two or three employees managed their franchisees' insurance files, and it just wasn't working for them.

We explained we could do a better job reviewing and tracking the certificates. Plus, we said if they hired us to manage their insurance certificates for them, they wouldn't need to hire new staff to ensure insurance compliance.

When Brand A accepted our proposal, we developed a web-based computer system with one of our original IT partners. Our system views the franchisor's FDD required coverages on the left side of the screen. Those are static coverages that are consistent among all of the locations, and they don't change throughout the year.

On the right side of the screen, we put the coverages that the franchisees were carrying at that particular time.

Every night, our system compares the required coverages on the left with the current coverages on the right. If they match, that location is compliant, and it's displayed in green. If they don't match, that location is noncompliant, and it's displayed in red.

Some situations that would be noncompliant—in red—are if the franchisee's workers' compensation has expired, if their general liability didn't have enough limits, if their automobile limits weren't high enough, or if their EPLI was nonexistent.

Once our EZCert program was created, we began sending Brand A monthly reports. Now they could tell each month which of their locations were in compliance—and which were not. They no longer had to call or email or pester all their franchisees for reports—only the noncompliant ones.

With the success of Brand A, we realized that regardless of the business/industry, every franchisor had the same insurance issues:

- The FDD is difficult to read.
- The insurance certificates are difficult to read.
- Most franchisees are required to buy several different types of insurance.

- The more locations they have, the number of insurance coverages grows—to an unmanageable level, requiring more and more people, time, and money to manage.

So, we started visiting other franchisors, and we discovered that many franchisors either did no tracking at all, or they were using same system that they started with when they had a few locations, but now they're at dozens or hundreds of locations and that system no longer works.

From there, EZCert began providing services to other franchisors. It eases the minds of our franchisors to know that we are working on their noncompliance at all times. They're relieved to get their monthly reports showing whether or not their stores are compliant on insurance. That's one less area of chaos that a franchisor has to deal with. And as we all know, chaos is bad.

And now, our upgraded EZCert system is available 24 hours a day, 7 days a week for you to review compliance with your franchisee anytime, in real time—on zoom, by phone, or even in person!

Here's how our five-step program works:

Step 1: Review the current insurance requirements of your FDD.

Step 2: Request the insurance certificates from all your franchisees.

Step 3: Organize and process the insurance certificates.

Step 4: Verify the compliance of the insurance certificates.

Step 5: Report to you on your franchisees' insurance compliance monthly.

We'll delve into the details of each of these five steps in the next chapter.

Our certificate tracking system is in place so people don't burn you. Our services ensure that the growing number of franchisees in your franchise are tracked, and ideally compliant, each month. Again, this means less chaos. And we do this at almost no cost to you, the franchisor.

An Abiding Franchisor

After starting our work with Brand A, we grew their compliance up into the 92 to 94 percent range. Please note, this doesn't mean that 6 to 8 percent of the brand is noncompliant. It means that it's not documented yet. Typically, in the month of renewal there's a two- to three-span in which EZCert has not yet received an incoming report from the franchisee and it's just not loaded in our system.

When a franchisor's compliance rate is north of 90 percent, we feel that the brand is adequately documented and the franchisees are usually covered correctly. 100 percent is very difficult to achieve because there's always at least one franchisee whose insurance is renewing tomorrow.

Unburdened by no longer having to track their franchisees' insurance certificates, the employees of Brand A were better off. Everyone could now focus on being a better hair-cutting business, and they were able to work on generating more revenue.

Unfortunately, tracking insurance on behalf of franchisee does not help a franchisor increase revenue. It does protect the franchisor from any insurance losses that could happen.

I believe that EZCert helped Brand A grow seamlessly and quickly. I will never claim that EZCert services brought them profit; that's not how compliance tracking works. Nor will I ever claim that we prevented any losses; retail in its entirety is constantly facing losses. My only claim is that we continue to keep Brand A free of litigation coming from franchisees across the country. That's our goal. It's what we do.

Brand A continues to be our shining example of how you can manage insurance compliance without needing to increase staff nor train current staff about insurance. By sub-contracting that work over to EZCert, Brand A was able to focus on growth and efficiency.

The owners at Brand A no longer needed to lie their heads down at night wondering when they might get sued because a franchisee has injured someone or damaged some property. EZCert gives them peace of mind.

CHAPTER 4
OUR FIVE-STEP PROCESS

STEP 1: REVIEW INSURANCE COMPLIANCE

If you as a franchisor contact EZCert, our first step is to meet with you. During that conversation, we ask about the kind of insurance compliance work that you're doing now. Are you currently complying with your compliance work on your FDD-required coverages? Do you request renewal insurance certificates from your franchisees each year? Every six months? Do you have a system to track your franchisees' insurance renewal dates?

Typically, brands say, "We have too much documentation flowing. We don't have anyone who understands the documentation, and we're concerned about our compliance on insurance. We're working with stores in California to New York, and we need to consolidate this information and organize it into a readable format that regular people can read."

When EZCert meets a new franchisor client, we look to understand their concerns. We know that more than anything, they worry about the financial protection of their assets. If a person gets injured or property gets damaged at a franchisee's location, an insurance claim can be filed, and they can even be sued.

Your attorney wrote your FDD insurance requirements on your

behalf, and you need to ensure that all of your franchisees are compliant.

The challenge is that FDDs can be cumbersome and difficult to read. Even though the FDD has a format each franchisor must follow, attorneys can write the information within those sections differently. So, once a franchisor contracts with EZCert to do their compliance work, we review the FDD to go over the insurance coverages that the brand is requiring.

At this time, we can share some insights into what we typically see businesses that are similar in nature do. Sometimes we suggest going back to their attorney to make adjustments on the coverage they are requiring.

In general, our goal in Step 1 is to do our best to explain and simplify the difficult subject of insurance into something that their staff can understand and work with.

Step 1 Worst Case Scenario: The worst case is no information nor request for renewal info on any franchised location, nor documentation of insurance purchased by any franchisee. This case is rarely found. However, I expect that some brands are in this position. The relative size of the brand and the amount of time exposed to public will dictate their risk for litigation. A thorough review of FDD coverages is required. EZCERT needs to get right to work, and our notifications will begin to show progress in short order.

Step 1 Average Case Scenario: EZCert typically contracts with franchisors in this position: A suitable effort was made to originate the required insurance at the closing or purchase of the franchise. Usually, a brand uses attorneys to handle all the appropriate documents in the sale of a business. Attorneys for both sides normally cross the insurance check box and all is well at the beginning. However, we run across a lot of closing when one party didn't hire an attorney, and in the effort to save money, some purchases are not done correctly. Limits are cut, and more importantly the language about additional insured status in favor of the franchisor is not verified. Far too often, franchisors accept affirmatives from the franchisee, yet they do not receive proof: certificates of insurance.

Upon renewal, franchisors expect their franchisees to renew their coverage as required. But they don't close the loop to confirm nor request copies of the insurance certificates.

Step 1 Best Case Scenario: Our best customer has hired staff to verify insurance across the brand, they have constant communication with locations, and they are fighting the battle themselves. There is time, effort, and cost involved here.

EZCert feels that we can do it more efficiently and consistently. A brand that is trying to handle their own insurance compliance faces staff turnover and staff education issues. It can be done, but we feel we can be more efficient. Staff should be used to help grow your brand instead of working insurance issues with locations. Ensuring that insurance is purchased across your brand is a non-revenue generating sport. It does not help your revenue line; it just saves you litigation from the field. Our best customer realizes how important this duty is and knows there just has to be a better way!

EZCERT has a solution for wherever your brand is on the compliance line, we can dig right in or just pick up whatever efforts you are currently doing.

AN ABIDING FRANCHISOR

Another brand, let's call them Brand C, came to us a couple years back. They found us through the International Franchise Association (IFA). At that time, they had around 650 locations across the country, and they were requiring four or five insurance coverages per location. At 650 locations, that's around 2,500 insurance certificates to track. They had documentable evidence that fewer than 10 percent of their franchisees were compliant on their insurance.

When they employed EZCert, we started by reviewing their FDD to learn what insurance coverages they required their franchisees to hold. Once we knew what their insurance requirements were for franchisees, we could get to work. Then we were able to set a framework for EZCert to input all the information on all the franchisees that Brand C had. We had taken the first steps together toward improving insurance compliance.

We've been able to improve Brand C up to about 61 percent documentable compliance—not the best, but also not the worst. Our goal is to get them up to 80 to 85 percent.

Brand C is an ongoing client of EZCert. We have done fairly well at Brand C in getting that compliance up. We've worked with them for about five years, and we were able to lower their losses. When losses come into the adequately insured franchisee, they never make it to the franchisor. We don't know what they could have been, but we know what they have been, and that's been a good thing for Brand C.

Currently we are in a new push phase to go after the franchisees who are not able to show documentable insurance. With the help of Brand C corporate, we'll email and call those franchisees, asking them to document their insurance coverages. Brand C has been a good case for EZCert.

Certificate tracking is an ongoing process where we have conversations with the home office, and we go through the next steps to take so they will be able to increase compliance to our goal. Brand C corporate is making a real push to improve their insurance compliance. EZCert can identify the franchisees who don't have insurance, but it's up to the franchisor to push the levers that they need to push to get those locations adequately covered. That process is still going forward with Brand C, and it continues to be a great partnership.

STEP 2: REQUEST CERTIFICATES OF INSURANCE

After reviewing a franchisor's FDD and assessing where the brand is currently with insurance compliance, our next step is to request all the insurance certificates.

To gather them, we call, email or mail letters to all franchisees and request certificates of all insurances required by the FDD. We inform them that their brand has subcontracted this work to our company, and we request current insurance certificates for all locations.

We always do our best to keep the communication positive while increasing compliance, with friendly reminders, such as, "It's a great day in your franchise's world. However, we need your new general liability certificate in the next 30 days because your FDD requires you to carry $2 million in general liability coverage."

It usually takes one to three months for us to receive all the certifi-cations. As we receive them, we input that information into our computer system. Then we can begin comparing the coverages required by the franchisor in the FDD with the coverages actually bought by the franchisee. This establishes a baseline of compliance for EZCert.

After we send those first letters or emails, we then send emails or letters notifying franchisees 90 days before their policies expire—reminding them to renew their insurance and to forward their new insurance certificate to us so we can maintain that file. For example, if a policy renews in December, that franchisee would have gotten their 90-day notice in September.

If a franchisee has six insurance coverages for one location, they don't always renew on the same day. For example, a franchisee's general liability insurance might renew at the time they signed their lease agreement originally in September, their worker's compensation might renew in January because they actually opened in January, and their umbrella insurance might renew in October because they purchased it while setting up for their grand opening. So, we send multiple letters to the same franchisee at those times in the hopes that all those coverages stay compliant.

If a franchisee doesn't respond to our 90-day letter, we then notify them 30 or 10 days in advance of their policy's expiration date. We can even notify them on the day of renewal if we haven't gotten their new insurance certificate.

If we're still waiting for renewal 10 days after insurance coverage expires, we will notify the franchisor directly. We'll explain that we've reached out to the franchisee several times, but we've not been able to secure a new insurance certificate. At this point, the franchisor must get involved to correct the issue.

To be clear, we don't want to reach that point. We want to gather the insurance information freely and easily in such a way that we don't have a conflict. We want the franchisee to maintain the insurance requirements on the FDD required coverages.

Sometimes, we discover that a franchisee's insurance agent doesn't know how to fill out an insurance certificate. EZCert can clean up that problem quickly, and we help to get a correct certificate of insurance.

Once the certificate of insurance is received by EZCert, we put it into the file for the franchisee and then we maintain that franchisee's insurance compliance on behalf of the franchisor.

If we realize that a franchisee is noncompliant because his coverages have expired or his limits purchases weren't correct, we can work with him to become compliant with insurance. We will help him because we want them to be compliant.

If a franchisee displays an unwillingness to work with EZCert, we will turn it over to the franchisor. The two of them together will then figure out a plan to get the franchisee compliant. Different brands handle their delinquent franchisees differently.

Step 2 Worst Case Scenario: The worst-case brands have no documented insurance file. No one has checked the renewal process, nor the opening process in a matter of years. Franchisees are not trained to provide the insurance required in the FDD. Lot of claims are flowing through the franchisees up to the franchisors, and things are just a mess. Usually coinciding with this this condition is a high churn rate of franchisees either selling or closing. Some guidance and order are needed. If insurance is being ignored, typically a lot of other issues are being ignored also.

Step 2 Average Case Scenario: Quite a few franchisees have current insurance purchased. However the franchisees are not forwarding their insurance certificates to the corporate office. Corporate is taking a hands-off approach to insurance, allowing the franchisees to purchase whatever they feel like. Consequently, some franchisees are considering the FDD as a suggestion, and there is not much follow through on the additional insured endorsements that can save a franchisor.

Step 2 Best Case Scenario: Our best-case franchisor system has staff dedicated to insurance compliance and has a grasp of the situation. Usually, some claims have filtered up the franchisor, and some claims have been paid. This brand is very easy to convince to subcontract this work over to EZCert—especially the employee charged with this duty, who likely has many other duties to manage. Working with insurance certificates is challenging, but this brand has a handle on what to do. They are just looking for a better way.

AN ABIDING FRANCHISOR

We met with Brand D at an International Franchise Association Convention in 2016. After a great conversation, we took them on as clients. At that time, they had 50 open locations. They had another 100 locations that were sold and in the process of opening. Each location was required to hold four insurance coverages, which has increased to five today: general liability, workers' compensation, umbrella, automobile, and employee professional liability.

On average, each Brand D franchisee runs 1.5 stores. Some have six, others have four, but very few franchisees have only one. Regardless, at 50 active locations, with four coverages each, they needed 200 total coverages, and when the other 100 opened, they would be looking at 400 more.

We officially reviewed Brand D's FDD soon after meeting with them. We found that their compliance was in the 10 to 20 percent range. It was then time for Step 2: Request Insurance Certificates.

Today, Brand D has 70 to 80 locations. At six insurances coverages per franchise, that's 420 to 480 total coverages. Together, we increased their compliance from 10 to 20 percent to around 75 percent. I think they're very happy with our service. Beyond the initial letters and the renewal requests, we continue sending monthly compliance reports, and we work with them to ensure the franchisees are adequately covered for the FDD.

Our system allows us and our franchisors to track all insurance coverages from all franchisees daily. The system compares their coverage against their required coverage every 24 hours. On any day, 90 days ahead of a franchisee's insurance renewal date, we're happy to remind them, "It's a wonderful day in Brand D world. You have a policy up for renewal soon." And we ask them to send their new certificates to EZCert so we can update and maintain their files.

We try to do all the leg work for our franchisors so they don't need to do it themselves. I spend a lot of resources on each brand, both in payroll and time, but the work must be done. Either the franchisor does it or we do it. And we think the franchisor is smart to delegate it to us.

STEP 3: PROCESS AND ORGANIZE

Now that we have reviewed, requested, and gathered all the insurance certificates, our next step is to process and organize them. We input the insurance certificates that we receive from all the franchisees into our computer system.

When you have a franchise system and multiple locations, a computer system is vital. Keeping everything on a yellow pad somewhere presents unnecessary challenges. We developed our computer system through trial and error, and it serves us well.

When we add a new franchisor into our system, that first snapshot can be eye-opening. Chances are good that there is no documented insurance because usually nobody was checking whether franchisees renewed their coverage or if they named additional name insured.

At this time, we compare whatever coverages the franchisees can provide us with their required coverages. Our system notes any coverages that are deficient in requirement, any note limits that are not high enough, any policies that are expired, and additional named insured information is missing.

How do we process and organize the insurance certificates? We can do it a few different ways. Sometimes we work state by state. For example, we'll start with franchises in Texas and get all the locations up and compliant, and then we'll go to New Mexico, and then to California.

Another way is by line of coverage. In other words, we can go through and check all general liability lines, then property lines, then workers' compensation, then auto, and then umbrella.

Whichever approach we use, the benefit to the brand is that this work is getting done—without them taking away time from their staff and their office. They can continue running their brand while EZCert is working the entire time, verifying the insurance compliance.

Getting a new franchisor started in EZCert system is a lengthy part of the process, but we get it done right the first time. After that, it's automatic. Once a client is started in EZCert, they can go back to growing their brand and growing their system—without worrying about their insurances.

One of EZCert's responsibilities is to maintain a back room file so that whenever a franchisor needs an insurance certificate from any of their locations, we can forward it to them right away—that day.

Step 3 Worst Case Scenario: There has been no work toward verifying that FDD required insurance has been purchased by any franchisee. The expectation level for compliance has been set at such a low level that the franchisees are not aware of its importance. Litigation against the franchisee that filters to the franchisor is usually what changes this.

Step 3 Average Case Scenario: Our average case is the franchisor knows he needs to have insurance more compliant, and he has tasked someone or some department with the duty. However, growth gets in the way of this monotonous duty, which needs to be done each and every day! When it is not getting done, EZCert offers a great solution.

Step 3 Best Case Scenario: Our best brand realizes the importance of FDD required insurance and maintains the compliance internally. They force compliance and review the insurance certificates as they come in. EZCert can keep up the compliance moving forward, and the brand can redeploy that labor pool to a more needy project for growth.

AN ABIDING FRANCHISOR

At the time of this writing, we had a visit with a bar-restaurant (70 percent food, 30 percent alcohol) we'll call Brand E. They're a fairly new operation in Louisiana. Brand E restaurants are big, 10,000-to15,000-square-foot buildings, and they can seat around 300 people at a time—significant restaurant operations.

A bar-restaurant brand like Brand E has a lot of opportunity for insurance claims to come in on the franchise side, so we definitely want to ensure that everybody's adequately insured. Restaurants can be a litigious area of our society. You have slip and falls, food poisoning, and the potential problems that come with serving alcohol, such as someone claiming that they were overserved before getting in a car accident. We need to ensure that the brand is protected, and that these people are trained in alcohol sales and delivery. That's what EZCert is here to do.

When we reviewed Brand E's FDD, we learned they had a pretty extensive list of insurance requirements. They had six different insurance coverages: property, liability, workers' compensation, auto, umbrella, and employment practices liability insurance. With an alcohol business such as Brand E, it's very important to have the correct alcohol liability coverage in place with a proper name of insurer. However, this type of bar-restaurant has a tendency to have claim issues and problems that should be covered.

When we met, Brand E had seven open franchises. Within the few months that we've been working with them, they grew to 12 locations. Plus, they have more than 100 sales for new restaurants coming soon around the country. While they only need to track 72 insurance coverages now, once those new locations are up and running, they'll have 600 coverages to track.

We reviewed their FDD, and once we contacted their current franchisees, we discovered that several of their locations had undocumented insurance. In other words, the franchisee indicated they *had* insurance, but there was no *documentation* on it. We advised the franchisor of this noncompliance, so they could rectify it with their franchisees.

After that, we began monitoring all of Brand E certificates as they come in, and we produce a report every month. We show them the compliance of any stores they have open, compared with the stores that are noncompliant. We hope to grow with this brand as they grow via more sold locations. They have a huge backlog on sold operations at Brand E, but these are difficult and challenging stores to get open because they involve lot of real estate, construction, and hiring people. It's usually a one- or two-year process to open a new store for them.

For us, however, once we have a brand in our system, it's very easy for us to add a new location. All we do is click "add location." It's that simple! We add the contact information, and we verify that the requirements are still the same. We then send the new franchisee a nice note saying, "It's a great day in Brand E world. EZCert handles the insurance compliance for Brand E. We'd like to work with you to get your insurance in the system so that we can monitor it as we go through the year."

It's truly an exciting time at Brand E, and their insurance compliance is much better today than when they had started with EZCert. Now their franchisees are about 90 percent insurance compliant. But because of EZCert, Brand E does not need to expend very much time nor effort in this endeavor.

STEP 4: VERIFY AND REVISE

Once we get a brand's franchisee used to dealing with EZCert, we can keep rolling compliance up higher, and higher, and higher. As explained previously, if a franchisee's insurance coverages are equal or greater than the FDD's requirements, it's listed on our system in green. But if a franchisee's coverage is not up to the FDD requirements, it's listed in red. (Red means stop, and green means go!)

In Step 4, we work through all the red locations to identify the problem: Have coverages expired? Are limits high enough? Was the named insured correct?

Overall, to the benefit of the franchisor, they're not having to use staff, time, or capital to verify whether the franchisee is covered or not. I tell brands all the time that certificate compliance work is a non-revenue-generating sport. Getting it done doesn't generate revenue for their brand, but it must be done. That's why EZCert is here.

At this point, we've requested, gathered, processed, and organized the insurance certifications. Now we need to report back to the franchisor to explain, "Out of your 800 locations, we have insurance compliance on 700. So, you have 100 locations around the country that are not compliant on insurance."

EZCert notifies the franchisor about those in-the-red franchisees because EZCert doesn't have the responsibility nor the power to force the franchisees to buy general liability insurance. All we can do is notify the franchisor if the franchisee is out of compliance.

We can help the franchisor try to gain that compliance by making phone calls and sending emails to the franchisees, but we have no power beyond communication and reporting. We're not trying to play tattle-tale on the franchisees. If a franchisee fails to purchase the required coverage or if she is unable to produce an insurance certificate, then she is not covered.

For a franchisor to tell a franchisee that they are not compliant and that they need to do something about it is a difficult conversation. It's important to note that the franchisee is a *customer* of the franchisor. Generally, calling a customer and adding work to their day is unpleasant, and it feels counter-intuitive to most business owners.

The uniqueness of EZCert is that we understand the relationship between the franchisor and the franchisee. We understand that the franchisee is a customer. We also understand that the franchisee is *supposed* to buy insurance. And we surely know that we must handle that situation delicately—and we do. I think that's what hinges this whole business.

But then what happens to the noncompliant franchisee?

A franchisor has a little bit of leeway in how tough they can be on a noncompliant franchisee who is not demonstrating that they have purchased the correct insurance.

For example, if the franchisee of a bar could not demonstrate that they had liquor liability insurance or that they established the franchisor as additional named insured, if I was the franchisor I would recommend shutting that bar down that day. I would not allow them to open their store with my flag hanging on the front porch.

Along the same lines, for automobile insurance, if you have a delivery-type company (like pizza restaurants), and they cannot document that they have delivery insurance for those automobiles, if I was the franchisor I would not let them operate. They could get into a liability claim and not have the correct coverage, and I would be the one who's hung out to dry.

These serious breaches usually are taken care of by the franchisor's attorney, with the ability to force place coverage! This means the franchisor can purchase coverage on behalf of the franchisee to protect all parties. It's very expensive insurance to purchase, but it can be done. Usually, the FDD gives the franchisor this power! If we arrive at this solution, the train has come completely off the rails, and we are just trying to survive.

AN ABIDING FRANCHISOR

EZCert sometimes reaches out to potential franchisor clients via email. We emailed Brand F out of Dallas, Texas, because they're a publicly traded company. Brand F operates stores in many areas of the country from California to Florida, renting things like furniture and TVs, especially to furnished apartment complexes. Brand F operates around 3,000 stores, of which 2,700 are corporately owned and of which 300 are owned by franchisees.

Brand F answered our email, and we made a trip up to Dallas to meet with them. After a great meeting, Brand F came onboard as a customer because they felt their insurance compliance work was inadequate. They didn't have the personnel to manage it, and they wanted to have a true certificate management system for their 300 franchisee locations. We were happy to have the work, and it gave us an opportunity to show another brand what EZCert does.

Upon reviewing their FDD, we found that their compliance was less than 10 percent—very low. In their particular case, we worked by state, emailing and calling franchisees and asking them to send in their insurance certificates. Over a period of a year or two, we were able to get their compliance way up to 50 to 70 percent.

Sometimes EZCert meets with franchises at their annual conventions. Doing this actually helps greatly with our communications with franchisees; we can introduce ourselves in person and tell them, "Hey, we're the EZCert people, and we're charged with the responsibility of getting your certificates of insurance." I think it makes everything much easier when people can put faces to a business or service.

Brand F invited us to their annual convention. When we met with them again, they let us know that the corporate operation liked how the franchisee division was performing as compared to their nonfranchise corporate stores. There was a big push to grow the franchise operation and have more franchisee stores and fewer nonfranchise corporate stores. We felt like we were a part of that success in getting their insurance compliance in line with a good system.

In 2018, Brand F sold their entire business—all corporate and franchisee stores. I think there's a big possibility that they hired EZCert to help them get compliance to be able to put the company on the market. We were so glad to hear that the company sold.

We have since stopped doing compliance work for the new owners of Brand F, but they were a good brand for us to work on. After receiving their good news, we moved on our way, and they moved on theirs.

STEP 5: REPORT

After EZCert has done its reviewing, requesting, processing, organizing, verifying, and revising, now it's time for reporting.

We always hope to have positive news for our franchisors. But when EZCert gives our report to your brand, you might need to take some steps to get that insurance back in place. When our reports fall on deaf ears, there is no enforcement action taken against stores without insurance compliance. Once that remains the case, it seems to run rampant through a system. One franchisee will tell another, "Corporate says you have to carry $3 million worth of liquor liability insurance, but we haven't, and nobody's gotten in trouble for it. So, we're just carrying $1 million."

I believe that a brand needs to enforce their FDDs in every way possible to keep the team aligned. If you're having insurance compliance issues with one franchisee, what other compliance issues might be happening there? Do they have cleanliness compliance issues? Staff compliance issues? Opening compliance issues? Usually if you have insurance compliance issues, it's just the tip of the noncompliance iceberg.

Usually, when people adamantly remain out of compliance, corners are being cut that don't need to be cut. The franchisee needs to hold the line and ensure they're adequately insured because insurance is what keeps you in business. Insurance keeps the royalty stream coming, in the event of some kind of property loss or liability loss. Insurance can get a store back up and running so much faster than a self-insured situation—where a particular location doesn't have any insurance at all. When a casualty loss happens, that process is slower than reopening and restarting that rule constraint.

A NON-ABIDING FRANCHISOR

Brand G is a restaurant and sports bar. I met them through some associates of mine. They were doing very well at the time, growing throughout the country. They were EZCert's third client. When they hired us, they had 60 franchise locations. We got the brand set up, and we found a fairly low documented compliance of 10 percent.

Much like Brand E, Brand G has a pretty high percentage gross sale of liquor. Liquor liability was obviously one of their required coverages, which involves extensive limits because of the amount of alcohol sold per location. So, it's a fairly complicated, sophisticated set of insurance. As I've shared, quite a lot of liability goes along with restaurants with high gross sales of alcohol. And its insurance is expensive.

Brand G's FDD was very well detailed, and it was fairly explanatory on what coverages were required. While the brand itself was great to work with, many of their franchisees ignored our letters of request. That led us to Step 5: Report.

We continued indicating to Brand G that there were locations of theirs without any documented insurance. Soon, even corporate stopped paying attention to the EZCert report, and they wouldn't follow up with their people about being in default. The compliance that we could document to the system was always fairly low, but we were able to at least increase their compliance from 10 percent to 25 to 30 percent.

Brand G grew over time. Over the next couple years, they went from 60 to 100 locations. Each one of those stores did somewhere between $2M and $4M. We couldn't get much traction on insurance compliance with very many of the store operators. And then, the brand itself did not take action with their franchisees. Brand G had the ability to force place insurance that they needed to. They had the ability to shut down a store for lack of insurance compliance. In our opinion, they wouldn't put the hammer down and hold people accountable for the contracts they had signed. Brand G ultimately failed, but recently they were able to sell their business.

EZCert has previously faced situations where the franchisee can't overcome a significant property, liability, or a liquor liability claim. We are there to ensure that these policies get renewed annually on behalf of the franchisees and to ensure there's a named additional name insured. When these things aren't taken care of or responded to, a brand opens itself up to litigation.

One incident at one franchise will filter all the way up to the corporation, and then attorney fees must be spent. The franchisor has taken their eye off the ball instead of growing the brand and creating a healthy situation. Now they're stuck with inadequate franchisees, and they're fighting litigation.

I personally think insurance compliance is a ball. I love what I do. My team and I understand that there are probably other issues in a brand—and that goes back to why franchisors should subcontract their insurance compliance out to a company like EZCert. We can give them advice when they're having issues with franchisees. But the franchisor is the one who needs to force place coverage. If not, they will lose control of their franchisees.

AN ABIDING FRANCHISOR

Brand H is a membership eyelash franchise where women can have their eyelashes worked on. The brand was started by a woman in California, and it's growing very rapidly.

I heard about Brand H around three years ago because franchisees in our EZCert system were buying into the Brand H franchise and letting us know about them. I made a telephone call directly to their CEO, then went to meet with her.

When we met, Brand H had 70 to 80 open franchises, and they had a total of 140 franchises sold. Sure enough, Brand H was having a very difficult time organizing their insurance compliance with their current franchisee locations—let alone the new ones coming aboard. They were running around 2 percent documented insurance compliance, and they had a pretty good array of insurance requirements in their FDD.

After visiting with them, they became an EZCert client, and we began organizing their insurances from their franchisees. We began the process of organizing insurance certificates, reviewing insurance certificates, and asking for insurance certificates around the country on the open locations.

As we went through Brand H's information, we were able to cut their employee burden on the insurance world as well as the cost of buying their insurance compliance. Three years later, they're now nearly 60 percent in documented compliance on the coverages required.

After Brand H's insurance compliance came up and they opened more franchises, they were sold to another owner. We take pride that their insurance is much more compliant today than it was three years ago. We were able to reduce litigation and costs for the brand, and they were able to sell the brand. Today, Brand H has grown from 140 open locations to around 200 to 250 locations. Their compliance increased from 2 to 60 percent with the new owners. EZCert is still able to do insurance compliance on behalf of the brand. I think we were very successful in helping them perform a duty that they had previously abandoned.

All around, Brand H really jumped. We attend their conferences where we regularly have a booth, and we remain happily involved.

AFTERWORD

I've shared our EZCert story and explained our simple five-step process. As you've hopefully gleaned, partnering with EZCert allows franchisors to subcontract the time and effort that goes into documenting insurance compliance per their FDD requirements. It is a payroll burden reducer. We can help any franchisor get their noncompliant franchisees into compliance, so they can continue growing their business and location.

Proper insurance coverage reduces the risk of litigation. And of course, litigation usually has a deterrent effect on growth. So, the more we can do to reduce litigation in a franchise, the better that brand can grow, produce results, and sell more franchises.

This is truly the end result that EZCert brings to the table. We are on the job every day, maintaining the insurance certificates on all the franchisees, and asking for the revision or the renewal certificates on all the franchisees.

Program Insurance Group

An additional benefit of working with EZCert is our partner, Program Insurance Group. Once we begin working with a brand, we are able to set up groups of people for buying opportunities. We deliver a better product price and a better product. By lumping all these brands in the same bucket, we're able to shop that insurance premium at the bigger number based on the number of locations in the system. Overall, we end up with better products, service, and control of the product. And we end up with a better insurance world that way.

Today, new franchisees know that there is somebody watching their insurance. They know that they can come to the Program Insurance Group, purchase insurance coverages for their stores, and access prices lower than those normally offered to them locally.

APPENDIX
INSURANCE ARTICLES

NEW FRANCHISOR INSURANCE Q&AS

Q: Most people know they need general and professional liability insurance and maybe even workers compensation insurance to open a business. But why are these so important?

A: First and foremost, a business is supposed to do the right thing and be socially responsible for its actions. This responsibility extends to the customers the business serves, but also to the employees who do the work. Making sure your business can defend a lawsuit from the general public for your actions or lack thereof is the right thing to do. The core principle of insurance is to pay a few small sums into a pool, so on the off chance an injury or fire happens, you can collect your total loss back from the pool. Having proper insurance can make the difference between a claim putting you out of business or protecting what you have worked hard to build.

Q: What's the most common mistake new franchisees make in regards to getting insurance?

A: New franchisees need to avoid under-insuring exposures. We most often see cases in which liability coverage has limits that do not protect the franchisee's personal net worth or new franchisees not purchasing umbrella insurance to extend limits and coverage. A new franchisee might evaluate policies solely on price because of the other spend involved in getting open as opposed to working with an experienced agent who knows the associated industry risks. Even if the Franchise Disclosure Document (FDD) of the franchisor is written correctly, making sure franchisees have independent coverage in place protects the brand and the franchisee at the same time. If a franchisee has a fire, is under-insured and cannot repair or rebuild, ultimately the franchisor and brand can be damaged. This is why brands should use a third-party insurance compliance company to verify, verify, verify. We use a proprietary tool called EZCert that helps franchises review franchisee compliance, which is critical.

Q: What are some other types of insurance extreme exposure franchise industries might need?

A: Typically, the policies are very much the same—general liability, property, workers compensation, auto, and umbrella—but the limits can vary drastically and so can coverage or even exclusions for an extreme exposure. Depending on the exposure, a much higher umbrella limit might be required, or errors & omissions insurance could be crucial for the work or service offered. It depends on where the risk is highest; ask yourself "what am I most likely to be sued for" and ensure your limits and coverage are more than adequate.

An independent agent will make sure policies are shopped across the market and not just one market. Rates can vary dramatically, so the agent needs to be familiar with your business. If the business is extremely risky or unusual regarding liability or property damage issues, a good agent will guide you through surplus markets. This is where an agent will advocate for you by helping you understand your special risk and the wording of your particular circumstances and needs. A knowledgeable agent can help secure and save your assets.

Q: Are there any new insurance needs because of the COVID-19 pandemic?

A: COVID-19, a pandemic of any sort, or large-scale natural disaster will have a long-term impact on the insurance industry as a whole. Traditional insurance is not designed to cover risks that could potentially expose every customer to a loss at one time, but there is still a need to have comprehensive insurance coverage as an important cost of doing business. All reputable insurance providers stayed current regarding legislation about waivers for liability exposures for customers and employers through the pandemic.

COVID-19 brought to light some types of insurance that are currently not as prominent as they might become in the future. With more employees working from home, data is being shared in completely new ways, and the potential for data breach, hacking, ransomware, phishing attacks, and the like has skyrocketed.

The insurance industry is also facing questions of how workers compensation will change for employees who work from home and might be injured on the job. Directors and officers insurance is also being looked at in a new respect after companies started questioning how their leaders and board of directors reacted to the pandemic. This topic is evolving daily and will likely see a great deal of activity over the next couple of years.

Q: What else would you like to tell readers?

A: Insurance, like many consumer products, is a cost of doing business in which you get what you pay for. If you experience a wide range of pricing among options, most likely the coverage you are reviewing is different. If the business is one that will not experience any losses, a franchisee could be fine with the lowest premium.

However, with almost all business, if there is a chance of loss through an employee, customer, vendor, or health and safety issue, it is critical to know your agent fully understands your business, you know who the coverage is with, and you are familiar with how claims are going to be paid. Franchisees should visit with their franchisor and with other business owners who are in their similar field to understand what can work best for them. They should also be confident in the insurance agent with whom they work, expect support as needed, reviews of coverage annually, and see the agent active within the franchise—even participating in annual meetings and conventions.

FRANCHISEES, IS YOUR COMMERCIAL PROPERTY INSURANCE UP TO DATE?

Franchises and property owners small- and large-scale are feeling the effects of increasing insurance rates across markets. These increased rates are a result of insurance company losses due to rising costs of building materials and overall replacement costs. Auto rates in particular are seeing dramatic increases. Changes in market conditions mean the monthly rate you secured when first purchasing a vehicle may no longer be sufficient to cover the actual cost to settle the loss. This inadequate pricing requires that rates be increased because auto insurance is based on an actual cash value policy. Whether you own a single car to take your kids to soccer practice or a fleet for your franchise use, learn how to adjust your policy to reflect changes in market behavior to ensure you are sufficiently covered in the event of a loss.

Hardening market

The trends we are seeing across the property market are a result of material hardening, that is, rates are being driven up by economic uncertainty and declining conditions. Market experts say conditions are only likely to become more drastic in the first half of 2023, as rates are expected to continue their climb. In times of market hardening, it is more important than ever to get ahead of disaster by ensuring your insurance policies have you covered.

How to calculate your needed coverage

While the auto market in particular is seeing dramatic changes, the market conditions can also affect other property policies. The co-insurance clause present in commercial and residential insurance contracts safeguards insurance companies by ensuring they get a fair premium for assuming the risk of loss. This clause requires a property owner to purchase 80 percent to 90 percent actual replacement cost coverage to qualify for replacement cost. If your home or property are underinsured, they will not qualify and they will become a co-insurer and will take responsibility for paying the remaining percentage in the event of loss. The customer and the agent are responsible for determining what the current replacement costs are for your market. True replacement cost can vary wildly for all markets across the country.

Consult a professional

While these steps can help find a starting point for insurance coverage, you should always consult with your agent for your specific needs and current coverage. To better understand your coverage and make necessary changes, take into account market fluctuations and consult with your insurance provider to make sure you and your business are covered and, in the event of an accident, you are not left responsible for more of the cost than expected. To protect your business, your customers, and even your personal property, a review of your insurance policies with a qualified provider is vital to ensuring variations in market behavior don't leave you vulnerable.

YOUR BIGGEST CYBER INSURANCE QUESTIONS, ANSWERED

In our fast and ever-changing digital world, keeping up with current digital demands can be challenging. Cyber-attacks are one of the leading causes of financial loss and affect more businesses each year. Every company is susceptible to cyber issues, even if it doesn't have a website. Cyber criminals can lurk in your systems for months without your knowledge and wreak havoc on decades of hard work in an instant. Protecting and preparing your company before a cyber-attack strikes is more important now than ever.

What Is Cyber Insurance?

Cyber insurance varies in type and size, but its intent is always to protect the insured's data, systems and servers. Coverage can protect everything from hardware to HIPPA to credit card information and more, as well as costs of monitoring required by law after a breach of cyber security. The most common cyber incidents that trigger insurance claims are ransomware attacks (files or devices blocked by hackers until a demanded ransom is paid), data breaches (confidential data is stolen or exposed), wire fraud (a scammer tricks an employee into sending money), and system failures (may or may not be malicious but cause costly system outages).

In addition to coverages, many cyber insurance providers include services such as forensics, breach coaching, and risk management offerings. In ransomware cases, a trained breach coach (usually an attorney) will have experience negotiating settlements and can often get the ransom request reduced significantly.

Why Is Cyber Insurance Important?

According to a report from IBM and Ponemon Institute, cyber security incidents are becoming more costly and harder to contain, with data breaches costing surveyed companies $4.24 million per incident on average. Cyber criminals do not discriminate between large and small companies. We often hear about cyber-attacks on large corporations, but many smaller companies end up paying thousands in order to get their systems, data and hardware back to safety.

Cyber criminals can be in and out of your systems for months undetected, leaving you exposed for long periods of time. Most server message block protocols are not prepared for a cyber event, so having insurance with experts on hand to help mitigate risk and restore your systems is invaluable.

What Do I Need in a Cyber Insurance Policy?

Cyber coverages are as unique to your business as they are to our IT-powered world. Some must-haves in your policy are first- and third-party coverage, and cybercrime coverage. Notice policy sub-limits on covered items, as well as waiting periods that often replace a deductible for business interruption coverage. Make sure to avoid coverage exclusions for not having the newest virus ware or updates. We recommend meeting with your insurance agent to discuss your company's greatest cyber insurance needs and to learn more about potential threats.

What Else Can I Do?

In addition to securing cyber insurance, protect your business from attack by using reputable vendors and training staff to spot scams. Ensure you are partnering with reputable IT vendors for your multi-factor authentication, electronic data processing, endpoint detection and response, and other cyber security needs. Training staff to spot phishing or scam emails and texts can make scams harder to perform and will help you stay on top of possible threats. Remember, good cyber security can help prevent an attack, but it's impossible to be invincible to cybercrime. Be ready to combat attacks with cohesive insurance coverage ready to deploy.

As business owners, we spend much of our time making sure we're prepared for anything, from weather emergencies to stock market changes to human resource concerns and more. Protecting technology shouldn't be an afterthought.

IS YOUR BUSINESS INSURED FOR A CYBER-ATTACK?

A critical piece of information for retail businesses and franchisees to consider is the exclusion of cyber liability from standard insurance policies. In fact, most don't even sell or offer cyber coverage. As reports of cyber incidents increase by the day, now is the time for every business owner to review their insurance coverage with their provider. The upside of this 21st century risk is the growing availability of tailored coverages and policies offering protection should a cyber-attack become a reality.

Here's a review of what is and isn't covered under typical property and casualty insurance packages for retail operations:

Most traditional property insurance excludes digital assets.

Regular property insurance is not designed for digital assets. Extended or fire coverage for the property is normally carried for real, physical assets such as furniture, office supplies, materials used in business operations, etc. Digital assets include items like documents, videos, logos, spreadsheets, and websites—any item that is stored digitally and has value.

Liability coverage is primarily designed to cover bodily injuries or damages to a third party, not a cyber occurrence.

General liability coverage is designed to pay on your behalf if your business is legally responsible for something done or not done that causes bodily injury or damages to a third party. Specifically, it covers the legal liability of a business for injuries or damage to any item of value, including anyone injured on your property or individuals who might require medical payments.

General liability insurance is also designed to cover personal and advertising injury, but not cyber-attacks.

Libel, slander, malicious prosecution, and copyright infringement are examples of personal or advertising injury and are typically covered under general liability insurance policies. However, cyber-attacks are excluded from the list.

It's important to note that a package policy or a business owner's policy is comprised of more than one coverage in a package.

No matter the size, all businesses are at risk of these exposures, and there has never been a more crucial time to understand them and research available options for protection. Cyber liability insurance is a specialized product designed specifically with cyber exposures in mind. Modern policies cover damages related to destructive cyber activity and are more comprehensive than ever before.

Commercial general liability insurance can pay for both first- and third-party costs associated with a cyber breach. First-party include costs associated with notifying affected customers and employees of a data breach, as well as investigating the source and effects of the breach.

Examples of first-party costs include:

- IT forensics
- Notification systems
- Credit protection
- Crisis management
- Crime and social engineering

Third-party costs cover the legal aspects of a data breach, including legal fees and settlement costs, civil awards, or judgments resulting from a lawsuit.

Examples of third-party costs include:

- Breach of contract
- Negligent protection of data
- Network security breaches
- Transmission of software viruses
- Denial of service attacks
- Defense of regulatory actions related to a breach
- Fines, penalties, and assessments

Here are four examples of actual losses paid by cyber insurance on cyber claims—examples most every retail business can find relatable:

Compromised Credit Card Data

Credit card data from several thousand cardholders was exposed through point-of-sale equipment. Cardholder information was stolen by hackers skimming payment terminals and then sold on the illegal market. When investigated, it was determined the business failed to maintain data security controls required under the Payment Card

Industry Data Security Standard (PCI-DSS). As a result, the bank-imposed fines and assessments against the chain totaled $275,000.

Employee-Activated Malware

In another instance, a network security breach of a credit union's computer network was compromised when a hacking group emailed a malware program to several employees. The malicious software allowed the hackers access to confidential data stored on the credit union's network and capture banking information for 20,000 customers and account holders. The total cost of customer notification, credit monitoring, digital forensics and legal consultation was $357,000.

Hacking a Stolen Laptop

A law firm partner had a laptop stolen from their car and the unencrypted laptop contained more than 10,000 client records that contained sensitive data, including social security numbers, medical records, and billing information. All individuals impacted had to be notified and were offered two years of identity monitoring. A total of $105,000 in expenses was incurred as a result of the stolen laptop.

Ransomware and Cyber Extortion

This type of combined attack recently happened to a medical office when a hacker entered the practice's network through unknown vulnerabilities, allowing them to install malicious software and encrypt personal health information, including patient medical records. The hacker demanded a ransom payment of five bitcoin to unlock the data. After a digital forensics investigation was conducted and the threat was deemed credible, the ransom payment was paid.

Today, most businesses are computer-reliant with files, information, and data stored digitally. To protect your business and customers, a review of your cyber exposures with a qualified provider is critical to ensuring your total risk is explained, mitigated, and covered should a cyber event occur.

Additional research and information have been supplied by Ashley Ganne, insurance broker with Brown and Riding.

IS YOUR BUSINESS LOCATION VACANT OR UNOCCUPIED?

"Vacant — many property policies contain a vacancy provision. Two similar terms—vacant and unoccupied—have specific meanings in the language of insurance and are defined in most policies. A vacant building contains little or no furniture or other personal property. Even if it is not vacant, a building can be unoccupied when people are absent. The wording in many property insurance policies limits, reduces, or entirely eliminates coverage when a building has been vacant (or, in some forms, vacant or unoccupied) for a designated period of time such as 45 or 60 days." – International Risk Management Institute, Inc.

An unseen result of the COVID-19 pandemic that should be a real concern to franchisees and small business owners is the understanding of whether your location is vacant or unoccupied. The pandemic had significant impact on businesses across the country in varying and different ways. While some businesses continue successfully operating, many have closed temporarily, and others have sadly closed never to re-open; we hope a majority will be up and running again soon. For restaurants and bars in particular, some have been mandated to fully close and some are only half-open or operating solely as to-go locations. As a result of these mixed scenarios, occupancy status for insurance purposes is something that needs to be on the radar of franchisees, licensees, operators, and business owners.

Most businesses have experienced effects of the pandemic and are working to innovate solutions. As insurance professionals, we often come alongside businesses and franchises in that innovation process and have discovered there is some confusion between what qualifies as "vacant property" and what is considered "unoccupied property" when it comes to coverage. This is proving true among many smaller franchised operations and privately owned businesses where there is less guidance as to how these issues can affect property insurance.

Property insurance, whether personal property or commercial property, normally has limitations on vacant or possibly unoccupied property as to fire, vandalism, burglary, theft and water damage. Each property insurance policy can and does read differently. It is critical to notify your insurance agent, in writing if possible, should your leased or owned property become vacant or unoccupied and the effective date of that status. Your agent will be able to analyze your specific policy and assist in determining the status of your property from an insurance standpoint.

Typically, unoccupied property describes a location that someone or a business intends to return to and vacant property is a property no one intends to return to. Your insurance agent can help you with either situation. In most cases, this condition of vacancy or being unoccupied can be triggered in as short a time as 30-60 days, but it is totally dependent on what the individual insurance policy says. Some coverages can be limited very quickly if utilities are not left on to protect property from freezing, mold, or water damage. Also important is the amount of furniture, contents, and products that remain in the building as a consideration for the insurance company to understand if the location is merely unoccupied or if it is deemed vacant. Your experience with an insurance company can go much more smoothly if your agent is kept current on your plans and actions, particularly if there is a claim or loss.

In commercial properties, percentages of tenancy can affect coverage, particularly if the property falls below 30 percent occupied, which is another reason it is important to notify your agent of your occupancy status. The agent can and should be able to counsel you about vacancy insurance waivers or recommend policies that are designed or written for this type of situation. If you are dealing with shuttered property, it is important not to make it worse by risking an uninsured loss and further financial hardship.

Our recommendations to determine the status of your property coverage are:

- Work closely with your insurance agent.
- If possible, keep the utilities on and monitor your location frequently.
- Do not abandon the property and keep contents in building until you have thoroughly reviewed the situation with your agent and landlord.
- Read and understand your coverage.

• Most importantly, notify your insurance agent of any changes of occupancy or change of use for a property.

Whether you own or operate a franchise or small business, this easily overlooked insurance issue can be a big problem or less of one if you take these actions now toward a more secure and successful future.

PREPARING FOR HURRICANE SEASON

On average, 17.7 hurricanes make landfall the United States each year according to the National Hurricane Center (<u>NHC</u>). Taking these steps now could pay off in the future of your business.

Prior to the storm:

• Review your hurricane plan before a storm is active.

• Know your emergency evacuation routes and share them with your team members.

• Keep travel clothing, water, and food packed and stored in an easy-to-reach location. Pack enough water and proteins to be set for a minimum of three days. Keep adequate amounts of batteries and gasoline for vehicles as well.

• While planning ahead of storms, review insurance policies to make sure you have adequate flood insurance.

• Take photos of your property to review at a later date if necessary. Store them on a cloud-based online platform, such as Google Drive, OneDrive, or iCloud, for easy access, particularly if needing to do so remotely.

• If possible, protect property from wind and flying debris prior to evacuation. Pay special attention to windows and doors.

• Invest in power sources, such as supplemental chargers for your devices, and maintain them.

• Stay up to date on National Weather Service bulletins via weather.gov or through local media outlets. You might want to consider investing in a NOAA Weather Radio receiver.

Avoid staying in an area after a hurricane evacuation advisory has been issued. Property and belongings can be replaced, but the health and well-being of people should be protected at all costs. It is important to predetermine how and when you will temporarily close your business and allow personnel to leave the area in plenty of time. There's typically ample warning prior to a hurricane event. Prioritize getting everyone away from the storm's path to safety. Once the area is deemed safe for return, use these tips to determine your next course of action.

After the storm has passed:

• While staying safe, take measures to protect your property from further damage, even looting.

• Notify your insurance agent of the status of your business and property and any known damages. Continue an open line of communication, when possible, with your insurance provider.

• Be careful around downed power lines and debris where there's often broken glass, other sharp objects, and other hazards.

• It is not uncommon for the aftermath of a hurricane to be as bad or worse than the approaching and active storm, so be mindful of potential flooding and tornadoes after the storm moves out of your area.

By creating and maintaining a storm plan, and following it when the need arises, you can be better prepared to help protect the individuals you employ, your family, and your business and property investments.

PREPARING YOUR BUSINESS FOR WINTER

Most people prepare their homes, cars, and families for possible hazards throughout winter. But taking critical steps now can help ensure your business is ready for whatever comes this winter and could pay off in preventing potential revenue losses due to weather. Planning ahead for treacherous winter weather will help your business brave the upcoming season with confidence. Here's how.

Have a winter storm plan. According to the National Weather Service, your primary concerns at home or work during a winter storm are loss of heat, power and telephone service and a shortage of supplies if storm conditions continue for more than a day. Prepare a plan for handling snow, ice, and freezing temperatures. Include everything from snowplow contractor contact information to employee and customer safety to closing protocols, and what to do if your employees can't get home.

Protect your pipes. Take steps to keep your business's pipes from freezing, especially if you'll be closing during extreme weather conditions. Disastersafety.org recommends sealing any building openings or cracks, running faucets, using a pipe monitoring system, and insulating pipes that are most vulnerable to freezing.

Winterize drive-thru windows. If you have them, make sure drive-thru windows are ready for cold temperatures. Perform any needed maintenance and consider installing air curtains to keep employees comfortable and windows condensation free.

Check HVAC systems and supplemental heating units. Have a technician inspect your HVAC system before any winter storm watches. If you have backup generators or other supplemental heating units, check that they ready-to-go if needed.

Communicate with your team. Share winter weather tips, storm plans, and safety information with your franchisees and/or employees. This is also a great time to make sure your internal communication software and tools are updated and working properly.

Double-check insurance coverage. There's nothing worse than realizing you don't have proper insurance in the middle of a weather emergency. Make sure you talk with your agent to know what coverages you have, coverage limits, and what additional coverages may be needed.

In any weather-related event, protecting people is most important. Keeping your family, employees, and yourself safe during winter weather is invaluable.

HANDLING PROPERTY AND CASUALTY INSURANCE PURCHASES OVER THE NEXT QUARTERS

For franchises and other businesses, it's time to dust off your reduce-the-risk hat for a while because insurance rates across the board are going to go up in price. Insurance companies had a tough 2020 and the two things that drive rates hit insurers hard in 2021—claims and capacity. Franchisees and franchisors will have to demonstrate to insurance providers that you are genuinely wanting to have fewer claims and run a tight ship to keep rates manageable.

Plenty of evidence signals rising claims running the gamut from weather-related events to COVID-19 exposures. Companies have been hit in all lines except Auto, General Liability, Employment Practices Liability Insurance, and Directors and Officers Liability. COVID actually cut Auto exposures but have drastically increased exposures everywhere else.

Another real factor is the financial situation affecting insurance companies—very low returns on their investment dollars mean they must make underwriting profits to survive. That's the capacity issue that could mean fewer insurance companies willing to take on marginal risk customers. Businesses, including franchises, must be able to demonstrate that the business is an above average risk to be able to demand pricing that is favorable.

The best advice is to know your agent well enough to be able to answer the following questions:

• Does your agent understand your business and your loss history?

• Does your agent support your business model or is it a representative who primarily offers generalized products to any willing buyer?

• If rates move up, will your agent work with you on a business plan to prove you're a good risk and will pay dividends?

If the answer to any of these questions is no, start looking now for a qualified agent. This environment is one in which franchisors will absolutely want to make sure franchisees have the correct and appropriate amount of insurance. If it's a growing franchise, small or midsize without the bandwidth to have a compliance officer, a franchise can benefit from a service like EZCERT to ensure the risk bearer is the responsible party in a loss and will be a valuable tool.

Now more than ever, it is critical to be more than an insurance buyer, it is time to make sure risk is reduced and that you're managing self-insurance and deductibles to put your business dollars ahead.

THREE REASONS IFA MEMBERS ARE TRULY STRONGER TOGETHER

I've been associated with the International Franchise Association for more than 15 years, and the majority of the companies we work with have been long-time members. Professionally and personally, membership has provided a learning platform and offers a pathway to meet others with shared goals.

I wish I had become involved in the organization sooner. Even though we worked with many IFA members, it wasn't until a decade ago we realized the value of the advocacy, leadership, training, and relationships that come with being involved and participating in the many programs the IFA has to offer.

I attended my first IFA Annual Convention seven years ago, when we were launching a service that supports insurance compliance for franchises. I went to the conference in New Orleans to look around at the trade show. I learned so much, made so many great connections, and left smarter as a result.

Whether in-person or virtual, great sessions and interaction with others who have meaningful real-world experience is of value to all of us in and around the industry. I've led roundtables in the past, and it is helpful to get to know what matters to franchisors and franchisees when it comes to what works for them in their unique, yet branded business. And the participants may have learned a thing or two about what they need to be doing to keep their personal investment in a franchise brand as safe and protected as possible from the discussions we had.

The outcome of membership and participation in all the IFA has to offer is lifelong friendships and partnerships, growth and development, and having fun along the way.

10 REASONS WHY AN INSURANCE REP ATTENDS THE IFA ANNUAL CONVENTION

There is great need among franchisors and franchisees to be compliant and fully covered for potential liabilities that are part of investing in and operating a franchised business. That focus brought me to membership in the International Franchise Association and, with that, attendance at the Annual Convention. Here are 10 reasons why:

1. I am not a franchise system, but being part of the IFA as a supplier gives me a chance to be together with current customers and meet potential clients.

2. l can meet and visit people to whom we answer as a supplier in one gathering rather than crisscrossing the country for meetings with each.

3. It's a chance to visit in person with all the folks I'm connected to on LinkedIn and a gathering of the brightest, most forward-thinking minds in the industry.

4. With a few nights in a hotel, I get to see and meet the new brands in development and bring them back to our team.

5. Getting to see my PR team that also attends the IFA Annual Conference and watching that team work fascinates me.

6. When we are out of the office and get to be with others in the industry, it's affirming that we are associated with some of the most powerful brands from across the country and around the world. Wow, we are fortunate!

7. I realize how special it is that we're able to travel now. Lockdown made us all appreciate the value of in-person gatherings.

8. Being able to satisfy a critical business need for a franchisor and its franchisees makes me want to work harder as a supplier.

9. The meeting is an opportunity to demonstrate to our team members ways we can grow our service reach through new, evolving, and existing franchise concepts.

10. Attending the IFA Annual Convention is a reminder of the value to be gained through shared learning and inspiration.

HOW TO AVOID RESTAURANT INSURANCE PITFALLS

The COVID-19 pandemic brought into focus what volatility can do to a restaurant's business. With so many unknowns, one thing is for certain: Restaurant owners, whether independent or franchisees, are going to have to be flexible and communicate well with employees to keep everyone as safe as possible.

Top priority for every restaurant owner right now should be ensuring their business is complying with Occupational Safety and Health Administration (OSHA) health and safety checks related to the pandemic as well as local and state regulations. It is also just as important to be mindful of your restaurant's insurance coverage to protect your business, personal finances, and your employees. Workers compensation insurance protects you from employee claims related to physical injuries and illnesses. Employment Practices Liability Insurance (EPLI) is a type of liability insurancethat covers wrongful acts arising from the employment process. The most frequent types of claims covered under such policies include wrongful termination, discrimination, sexual harassment, and retaliation. Restaurant owners should protect themselves with EPLI for these types of claims and possible litigation. Along with insurance coverage, be sure you are:

• Implementing effective hiring and screening programs to avoid discrimination in hiring.

• Posting corporate policies throughout the workplace and placing them in employee handbooks so policies are clear to everyone.

• Showing employees what steps to take if they are the object of sexual harassment or discrimination by a supervisor, making sure supervisors know where the company stands on what behaviors and those that are not permissible.

• Documenting everything that occurs and the steps your business is taking to prevent and solve employee disputes.

• Recording the ways your company is complying with safety practices and potentially going the extra mile for customer well-being.

If your restaurant is going to have a change in employee counts, make sure your insurance coverage fits your footprint and that it has been reviewed by your attorney. Additionally, secure a close relationship with a reputable HR company; many EPLI carriers offer resources in this area included with the policy. If you normally purchase Errors and Omissions (E&O) and Directors and Officers Liability (D&O) insurance, be prepared to answer quite a few more underwriting questions in the future. Rates will likely rise because of claims, and there could be a smaller number of suppliers for these lines of critical business insurance.

Specific to franchises, the Franchise Disclosure Document (FDD) requires franchisees to have insurance coverage, but not all franchisees are up to date after COVID-19 business disruptions. This can leave franchisors particularly vulnerable if there's not a person, department, or service like EZ CERT to monitor compliance and help protect the brand. Make sure you are working with an insurance representative who best understands the ebbs and flows of your restaurant business.

A quick review of EPLI-type claims:

Gender discrimination: A national restaurant chain paid to settle a gender discrimination lawsuit brought by men alleging they were denied more lucrative server positions because of their gender.

Retaliation: A server is given a "last chance" warning about coming to work late. The disgruntled employee immediately makes a complaint to the health department about alleged unsanitary food-handling practices. Upon being terminated for coming in late again, the server alleges the firing is in retaliation for making the complaint.

Sexual harassment: A restaurant franchise was forced to settle a sexual harassment claim by several teenage workers who alleged the manager behaved inappropriately.

Fair Labor Standards Act: Several salaried assistant managers in a mid-sized restaurant chain filed a class action lawsuit alleging that being required to perform occasional "non-managerial tasks" — such as bussing tables, running the cash register or serving customers — qualified them as hourly employees and therefore entitled them to overtime pay. The court granted class action status to the group of former that cost the chain more than $1.3 million to resolve.

Third-party ADA claim: A customer threatens to file a class action lawsuit alleging a restaurant is not Americans with Disability Act (ADA) compliant. The customer and their attorney often settle for a "bargain" of $15,000 to $20,000, knowing defense costs for a restaurant could reach six figures.

These examples are not exhaustive, just a quick overview of some of the cases making headlines. Every restaurant owner or franchisee needs to update insurance coverage and take the time to review policy coverage to avoid pitfalls that could impact their restaurant.

SAMPLE CERTIFICATE OF LIABILITY INSURANCE

ACKNOWLEDGMENTS

This book came about a year or two before the COVID-19 pandemic, and it was a joy to think about what we do for franchise brands and how we go about earning a living! Getting thoughts down on paper could not have been possible without the generous help and encouragement from Jennifer Bright because her enthusiasm was contagious.

Special thanks should go to my good friend Gordon Logan and his team at Sport Clips whose support and business is vital to our team. Sport Clips has allowed us to try out theories and practices to hone our craft with no embarrassment because of our failures! Thanks also go to Tropical Smoothie, Rent-A-Center, Nektar Juice and Tilted Kilt, who have always supported our team and have allowed us to grow in confidence!

I truly appreciate it!

ABOUT THE AUTHOR

Doug Groves is the force behind Program Insurance Group and its affiliate EZCert Management. Doug has more than 30 years of experience in the insurance industry. With his multifaceted background as an Area Developer for multiple franchises, Doug brings the expertise of the franchise industry to Program Insurance and Certificate Management Services. He maintains ownership in two insurance agencies and continues to do franchise development. He has a wife, three adult children, and is an avid outdoorsman. Doug is passionate about philanthropy and is filled with an entrepreneurial spirit. He can be reached at doug@pigbcs.com.

FOR MORE INFORMATION

Visit EZCert at www.certmgmt.com or call 844-744-7526.

Visit Program Insurance Group at www.pigbcs.com or also at www.programinsurancegroup.com or call 844-744-7526.

Beyond working with our franchisor clients and generating their reports, EZCert also writes articles once a month for the brands about exposures that they have and the coverages that are available for the franchisees to purchase. We want our clients to know what's going on and what they need to do to protect their businesses.

Our franchisor clients are like family. Once we start doing EZCert work, we end up meeting the franchisees across the country. We attend their conferences and trade shows.

Together, EZCert and Program Insurance Group stand ready to help your brand grow—both in insurance compliance and in satisfaction with your franchisees and their insurance programs. Over time, you can lower costs, improve coverage, and reduce the amount of claims for your brand.

EZCert and Program Insurance Group stand ready to help you maintain your insurance compliance throughout the year on all your locations—quickly and seamlessly.